Plainsongs

Editor

Eric R. Tucker

Associate Editors

Becky Faber, Michael Catherwood, Eleanor Reeds

Editors Emeriti

Dwight Marsh, Laura Marvel-Wunderlich

Publisher

Corpus Callosum Press

Cover photo by Chris Goedert

Corpus Callosum Press
Hastings, Nebraska

Subscriptions to *Plainsongs* are $25.00 annually for two issues, published in January and July. Subscriptions can be purchased online at the Corpus Callosum Press website.

Plainsongs welcomes submissions. The manuscript deadline for the Winter 2022/23 issue is June 15, 2022. Contributors will receive one free copy of the issue in which their poem appears. For each issue, the Board of Readers will select three poems to be honored as award poems. Award poem winners will receive a small monetary amount, currently $50.

Please use our online submission manager, available at the Corpus Callosum Press website, to submit work. Though we will endeavor to consider all e-mailed and snail-mailed submissions, we cannot guarantee responses for work submitted via these methods. Non-submission-related correspondence can be e-mailed to etucker@corpuscallosumpress. com or mailed to Corpus Callosum Press, PO Box 1563, Hastings, NE 68902. For more information about submitting poetry or subscribing to *Plainsongs*, please see our website: https://www.corpuscallosumpress.com/ plainsongs.

Cover photo by Chris Goedert.

Plainsongs is indexed by Humanities International Complete, EBSCO Information Services, 10 Estes Street, Ipswich, MA 01938.

ISBN-13   979-8-9853780-0-9

ISSN 1534-3820

Plainsongs

Winner of the Jane Geske Award,
presented by the Nebraska Center for the Book

Notes from the Editor

Welcome to issue 1 of volume 42 of *Plainsongs* poetry magazine. We're so pleased to have you with us. Within these pages you will find award-winning poems by Riley O'Connell, Ellis Elliott, and Darrell Petska, accompanied by insightful essays written by our dedicated associate editors, the poets Eleanor Reeds, Becky Faber, and Michael Catherwood. In the pages beyond, you will discover seventy-six additional poems by seventy-six other talented poets from across the United States and around the world—a cavalcade of songs by friends old and new to help you usher in the new year. The striking cover photo of a sunset in Smith Center, Kansas, by the artist Chris Goedert sets a reflective tone as we look back on the messiness of the year that was—with its parade of joys, pains, successes, bafflements, and challenges—and look ahead to the promise (and, let's face it, ongoing challenges, bafflements, etc.) of 2022.

I want to take a moment to acknowledge associate editor Becky Faber for being awarded the 2021 Mildred Bennett Award, which recognizes individuals who have made a significant contribution to fostering the literary tradition in Nebraska. Congratulations, Becky, on this well-deserved honor. We are so fortunate here at *Plainsongs* to have Becky, Eleanor, and Michael on board as associate editors. We simply could not do this work without their expertise and support.

We hope you enjoy the winter issue as much as we enjoyed putting it all together. Be well and stay safe. We wish you much joy, peace, and poetry in 2022.

Eric R. Tucker
Hastings, Nebraska

Contents

Self-portrait as the things we put inside us

Unremarkable as he was,
        I remember his wife
was on her third baby
of Biblical sobriquet
in as many years
and he was pulling out
        his demerit book
because of a fifteen-year-old girl's
        Old Navy shorts. Then our messiah

whip-smart, tampon pulled out
        of a pencil bag and cast across
the classroom like money changers'
tables in the temple courts
like a Pharisee trying to get in
to the kingdom of Heaven
        and I said thank you Jesus
thank you for dying
        so we could live

to see a grown man forget
        to punish a girl for having legs
due to the irreverent revelation
of a swathed cylinder of cotton
leaping and genuflecting
before his lectern. But of course
        this poem isn't about tampons
or my mom making me
        a truant on days they paraded

anti-Planned Parenthood pregnancy
        propaganda or the columnist-
evangelist youth group leader decrying birth
control as "an abortion every day."
Please God, not another poem about falling
out of feeling with the church
        the bride of Christ, the only woman

I was ever trained to love.
          More about my bewitching

bath tonight: salts, suds, goji
          tarocco orange. Between pages
of Ross Gay and the satin breaths of
ASMR, I feed myself pasta
salad, noodle by noodle
like old royalty, like new woman
          like God herself incarnate.

Riley O'Connell
San Mateo, California

About "Self-portrait as the things we put inside us": A Plainsongs Award Poem

Riley O'Connell sets the tone of this poem's "irreverent revelation" quickly with the unexpectedly wry and precocious term "sobriquet" in only the fourth line. While the anecdote that occupies the first half of the poem is a familiar complaint about the patriarchal practice of school dress codes, the cleverness of our narrator and the specificity of her descriptions make it feel fresh. Clearly the speaker is as "whip-smart" as her "messiah," a fellow student who disrupts a male teacher's religious hypocrisy by throwing a tampon in a gesture akin to Jesus upturning the "money changers' / tables in the temple courts."

The first two stanza breaks are stunning in their reclamation of Christ's sacrifice and radicalism, now embodied in an everyday act of feminist rebellion. I cannot help but share in the sincerity of the speaker's gratitude as she thanks Jesus "for dying / so we could live // to see a grown man forget / to punish a girl for having legs." The prosaic simplicity of O'Connell's language in such statements is complemented by its evocative aurality elsewhere as, for instance, the "swathed cylinder of cotton" is described as "genuflecting / before his lectern."

The poem contains a volta in its central stanza as the speaker reassures us what "this poem isn't about," aware that we might also roll our eyes at "another poem about / falling out of feeling with the church." O'Connell offers us a celebration rather than a rejection, an invocation of an alternative form of faith centered in the sacred feminine. The speaker revels in the sensory pleasure of a bath, "salts, suds, goji / tarocco orange," as she feeds herself. This is, after all, a "self-portrait as the things we put inside us" so it is not only tampons but pasta salad enjoyed "noodle by noodle" that we are asked to imagine as symbols of bodily autonomy.

This poem discovers the divine in the bodies of women more often asked to submit to a desexualized procreative role. As it concludes, the self-nourishment and self-care of the speaker demonstrate her likeness to "God herself incarnate."

Eleanor Reeds
Hastings, Nebraska

Instructions on How to Be a Stepmom to a Disabled Son

Take one 8-ounce can vanilla PediaSure, viscous brown, and
    smelling of old milk
and dryer sheets. Mix with microwaved Quaker oatmeal, cooled by
    two ice cubes. Stir.

      Lift open the kitchen window, let the pine tree's green breeze
        ferry the aroma.

Fill the barrel-like cylinder of the syringe, and take your time,
    pulling slowly. Watch the thick
liquid rise. Tie the Carolina blue terry-cloth bib behind his neck.

      Check the roman numerals on the blue circle of clock,
        estimate when to push
      his wheelchair outside for the bus.

Attach the graying feeding tube to the valve above his belly button
    that looks
like those on bright-pink inflatable swim toys.

Fill the syringe. Empty. Fill the syringe. Empty. Finish. Pull the
    tube. Close the valve.

      Close the window, place Grand Meme's quilt around his
        shoulders.

Stroke his stubbled jaw. Test the electric razor on the back of your
    hand. Hold his head
in one hand to keep him still, use the other to shave.

      Kneel in front of him. Cup his curved, bare foot to pull up
        his purple Vikings sock.
      Wrestle on a black Converse high-top, and lace up.

Push him out the kitchen side door as the bus lift makes its slow
    slide to the ground.

Ellis Elliott
Juno Beach, Florida

About "Instructions on How to Be a Stepmom to a Disabled Son": A Plainsongs Award Poem

When my children were small, I often relied on Dr. Spock's *Baby and Child Care* to help me with the ups and downs of parenting. I faced nothing like the responsibilities of parents of children with physical or developmental challenges, especially if they lack ready access to resources.

In this poem, readers are brought into the realm of a nonbiological parent dealing with the process of tending to an older child who cannot perform tasks for himself.

The clarity and precision of each stanza bring an openness to the reader to be not only a close observer, but also a co-participant. Through these instructive verbs, *Take—Lift—Fill—Check—Attach—Fill—Close—Stroke—Kneel—Push,* the physicality and frequency of tasks unfold. I admire the tightness of each instruction and the way a rhythm is developed. The use of alliteration as well as the use of colors (*viscous brown, graying feeding tube, bright-pink inflatable swim toys, purple Vikings sock, black Converse high-top*) deepen the delivery. These step-by-step instructions prompt the reader to ask how this stepmom learned the process—were there instructions for her to follow? Being a caregiver is an exhausting responsibility, and every day would be filled with these tasks. The poem's clear actions of hands and eyes and heart combine to make this an emotionally engaging piece.

This poem shows what parents/caregivers handle each day, not only the tasks that they must complete, but also the trust that they invest in others, such as the driver of the bus with the lift who comes to pick up this young man.

The writing is tight, and the language is visually perfect. I am a better person for having read this poem.

Becky Faber
Lincoln, Nebraska

Days Before Time

Up to their porch we'd run
toward hugs smelling of yeast breads
and sweet pipe tobacco.
Candies hid in their pockets: *guess which?*
Well-loved toys and tattered books
spilled from boxes in the corners.

They'd tease, tell stories, play games.
We helped bake cookies and cakes
and climbed the trees out back.
When we had to leave, clutching goodies,
they'd stand at their door and wave
as we waved back.

They'd always be there—
Sundays, holidays, any time at all,
ready to laugh, ready to share,
always smiling and hugging, always saying
I love you and waving as we drove off
in those days before time came to town.

Darrell Petska
Middleton, Wisconsin

About "Days Before Time": A Plainsongs Award Poem

In Darrell Petska's "Days Before Time," the reader is treated to objects, smells, and tastes that trigger pleasant memories of visiting Grandma and Grandpa's house. Characters in the poem are revealed by the joys that greet the visitors.

As the poem first greets the reader, the grandparents are "hugs smelling of yeast breads / and sweet pipe tobacco." There are "toys and tattered books / spilled from boxes." Universal appeal of a poem has no secret rule or ploy; it is simply sincerity, and there is a plethora of depth from Petska.

"Days Before Time" reaches both children and grandparents through restrained grace. And Petska produces three stanzas of genuine emotion and tribute. Sensory images and objects carry the weight of character: "They'd tease, tell stories, play games. / We helped bake cookies and cakes." A loving tribute flows from the poem, and when they "had to leave… / they'd stand at their door and wave /as we waved back."

The emotional pivot in the poem comes in the third stanza: "They'd always be there—"; there is a list: "Sundays, holidays"; "ready to laugh"; "always saying / I love you." Then the devastating final line of the poem: "in those days before time came to town." There is no need to explain how time changes all the characters in Petska's wonderful poem; its understatement carries with it the sincere depth of its weight and loss.

Michael Catherwood
Omaha, Nebraska

There All Along

We found the gifts, tucked in the bottom of our father's closet,
the one with the plywood doors painted white that slid
from one side to the other, the ones that hid the secret door
to his office. The gifts were tucked behind his scuffed yard shoes
and black work shoes and below all those hanging suits
and we couldn't help ourselves, being six and eight,
or eight and ten, or ten and twelve—who knows how young
we were but we wanted to know what Christmas would bring
and maybe that was the first time I thought that knowing
a thing before it happened was better as I pulled off box lids,
as I peeled away tissue paper, as the truth revealed itself months
too early. Years later I wanted to know *will I get cancer, will you
love me forever, when will each person I love die, when will I,*
none of which I could possibly know ahead of time, except
for that you wouldn't love me forever.
I think I knew that all along.

Shuly Xóchitl Cawood
Johnson City, Tennessee

COVID Nights

A year and a half has passed when my mother finally
calls to arrange a meeting at the Citizen Hotel in Sacramento

and also in Cesar Chavez Park, locales shifting
back and forth between us, as if we were balancing on an existential

bongo board, neither here nor there but somewhere.

She's young still, late 30s, severe beauty, hood of coal-black hair
setting off the smoldering angles of her face, a scowling Joan of Arc.

She's bundled in the same chic white coat she wore
outside Jerry and Johnny's the spring evening of my father's

40th birthday, the night he collapsed on Third Street
defeated, clasping a bottle of Glenlivet, surveying

the long astonishment of her legs.

She sits across from me at a table for two. It's spring again,
the world approaching the event horizon.

As always, she takes her coffee black.
She's not wearing a mask.

It's a pandemic I say, offering
her a KN95 pulled from my back pocket.

She lights a Kool menthol, exhales.

What do I care? she says. *I'm dead.*

I twitch and shudder, erratic weight pressing down on my chest.

She flicks her ash, carries on—*I pray for the day*
I no longer have to put up with your shit.

Smoke burns my eyes, snakes down my lungs.
Hapless, I, too, am without a mask.

We're in a huge ballroom, empty save
my mother and me, walls ruched in ivory satin.

Panicking, I push back from the table, beg off—
No time to say hello, goodbye.

She waves me away with her cigarette.
She can't be bothered.

And then I'm sprinting through Cesar Chavez Park,
packed with revelers, a smash of trombones and
saxophones bellowing the blues. So much spray and spit.

Not one soul is masked.

I tug my shirt up over my face, and I'm trying
to outrun it, whatever *it* is, until I can no longer
bear it, legs giving out, head lolling between my knees.

It's dark now, the sky choked with stars. A wind
ghosts through the city corridors, cindersong of the living,
motherdust of the dead.

Moira Magneson
Placerville, California

The Cover Up

Every year it was one of the most stolen books from the Tulsa library system.
Every year I would send them a new box.
　　Scott Ellsworth, author of *Death in a Promised Land: The Tulsa Race*
　　Riot of 1921

In the late fifties I was teaching history
at Booker T. Washington High in Tulsa
when I told my students
about the massacre in 1921.

"The whites came over the tracks,
machine guns blazing, wiped out Greenwood,
probably more than three hundred dead."
In fact, I told them, they'd used this building,
Booker T. High, as a hospital for colored folks.

"I don't believe that!" one of my students shouted,
a pool hustler named Don Ross.
"How come don't nobody know nothing about it, Mr. Williams?"

But I remember. I was sixteen,
fighting next to my father,
trying to save our building, our business,
Williams Confectionery, down the block
from our other business, Dreamland Theater,
corner of Greenwood and Archer.

The whites finally overwhelmed us.
They marched me down Greenwood,
my arms reaching for empty sky.
I watched a white boy running from our house,
a fur coat belonging to my mother
clutched to his chest like the pelt
of some animal he'd just killed.

Next day I showed Don Ross the pictures,
charred corpses and burned-out buildings,
took him to meet other survivors.
How come don't nobody know nothing?

I told Ross: "Because the killers
are still in charge of this town, boy."

Charles Rammelkamp
Baltimore, Maryland

Opening

The spirit of sparks descends, light licking
The white folds of the window, breaking the bonds
Of air and walls, bringing birds and the sounds

Of crickets, flinging the first and prickly pinecones
Of the sun season headlong into the hot
And damp domain of every house,

Whistling past the threefold threat
Of propriety, perfection, and purpose,
Delaying the destination until only the way

Remains, unreasoning in its untiring openness.

Kate Deimling
Brooklyn, New York

Picking Season

That candle you bought smells like apple cinnamon,
so now I am sad because desert living means no
orchards to pass like years ago on my commute
home from a college sometimes boxed by corn,
other times flush with the horizon. When the days
darkened at four o'clock and I layered tights
under socks under more socks, I would follow
my breath to our parked car and once belted,
relegate my direction to the upper windshield,
pirouetting geese my guide to Lincoln Highway.

I always felt like I was in a *Peanuts* special
expecting Charlie Brown, after Lucy pulled
the ball his foot was meant to kick, to land
in the pile of leaves outside my window,
and I craved a crayon, a hand turkey I might
outline after uncurling my fingers from
the steering wheel. I liked those
drawings adorning our school gym,
especially the night of the Sadie Hawkins
Dance when over the beats of "Rock
Lobster," Randy, the fifth-grader
I'd asked, told me he liked
my striped turtleneck and corduroy
jumper, the two of us leaning against
the cider donut table, cinnamon
and nutmeg wafting. Tonight,

though, I stand below the chili pepper
poster we framed our first year here,
watch you at the stove, our desert
windows discharging any Midwestern
pomp, circumstance, or celebration,
as a small flame enclosed in a cold
jar, spices
our fluorescent-lit kitchen.

Amy S. Lerman
Mesa, Arizona

Black Dog

You might meet us on our nighttime walks.
I'll be the one
        shouldering the wind,
        behind my old bête noir—
                an unkempt, hulking something
                like the shadow of a direwolf,
        nosing through each pile of trash
and tugging at the lead.

He speaks in landscape—mostly
through his power of selection. He loves
        the moonless waterfront, shuttered nurseries,
                those hilltop neighborhoods
                where ivied mansions
        crouch behind high gates,

and bridges, always bridges—as if to say:
the points of land these blind
        dumb girders leap between
        are more connected to each other
                than you are now (or yet will be)
        to any other human being.

When, I wonder, will the day arrive
When I can finally claim
        to live without regrets?
        Where is the calamity
                Of which I'll one day boast
        "It was the best thing
that ever happened to me"?

Perhaps an ancient waitress will appear
In that greasy spoon I always find at four AM
        My life to order on a tray (with a side of toast)
                She'll eye my grim familiar,
                shake her head, and say
        "You can't bring that thing in here.
        I'll wrap your food to go."

Halfway home I'll think of where
I've seen her once before:
        Another nighttime stroll, another
        wharf or bridge, her own rough cur—
                all yellow eyes and matted fur
                as black as rain on asphalt—
                        nipped her heels and tugged her toward
                        the wide and rippling darkness.
                She caught my eye,
                returned it, sighed,
        and vaulted from the railings
        with a smile on her face.

Christian J Cacibauda
Reno, Nevada

Bad Connection

On the other end
of the line, he clears
his throat. Nothing
to say. Years ago,

he lifted her
to the ceiling,
let her run her fingers
against its bumps.
They laughed,

the noise far away
now, like a crevice
between them
has ruptured
into a canyon.

She pictures it:
Fingers coiled
against the brim
of her hat,
turkey vultures
spiraling overhead.

Some part of her
still hoping
for a wave
from the other side.

**Natalie Schriefer
Trumbull, Connecticut**

The Farm Forgets It Was a Farm

The loft barn wears the same ash gray sweater
every day, with elbows worn thin where boards
are missing. Brush and briars fill the garden,
and fencerows grow unruly like untrimmed
eyebrows. No one visits. Strangers glance
in as they hurry past. The doors stand open,
and the fences are down, but there is nothing
to keep in and no reason to keep anything out.
In the unmown fields, winds with no place to be
make a muffled uncertain shuffling sound
like his stocking feet lost in his numbered hallway.

Phillip Howerton
West Plains, Missouri

Double-A Ball at Dudley Field, El Paso, 1980

You can hear the girl
who's going to do the National Anthem
singing scales in the home team dugout
while the starting pitcher is warming up.
You can feel the spray
when the lone groundskeeper
hoses down the infield.

Scoring is liberal—
I've never seen so many balls
become so intimate with the leather
and still get called hits.

In straightaway center,
there's a freak of design
the near-equal of the Fenway's Green Monster
or the cigar-box bleachers in the old Polo Grounds—
a green-sided alcove as long, front to back,
as the antipodal trot from home plate to mound,
the turf pitching upward on an eight percent grade.
A drainpipe runs under it,
humping water from the Franklin Mountains
down to the Rio Grande,
if only by the drop.
I once saw Tom Brunansky
stagger up that little hill
in the late innings of a game with Shreveport,
chasing a deep fly ball
but looking more like a man
trying to stand up in a rocking chair.
He let it fall in.
I think Alan Wiggins hit it.

After the game,
it doesn't take long
for twenty-five hundred people to file out.
Shutting Dudley Field for the night
is about as easy as closing a small-town drugstore.

You come home from Dudley
just like the ballplayers—
red dust in the hollows of your eyes.

Vincent Ercolano
Baltimore, Maryland

Phantom Dwelling

Basho said, *In the end we all live, do we not, in a phantom dwelling?*

Early mid-February morning.
Cool wind and moon-glow on the water.
Gemini at sixty degrees and Scorpio rising.

No bird wings yet ruffle the air.
No sound save water ripple.
This isn't loneliness; this isn't heartache.

This is the joy of being in a phantom
dwelling, breath visible on the air,
heart surge and lung heave,

the sweetness of wandering alone
through the countryside of self, lost
in the hushed wilderness of thought.

Frank Jamison
Kingston, Tennessee

High Dive

Up here
is closer to heaven,

and down there
under the water

is closer to the grave.
That brief second

while you're falling
must feel something

like death—
the butterfly

in your stomach,
the jolting clap

and sting
of your re-entry.

All the kids lined
up behind you watching—

one of them crying,
another

holding her breath.

Dave Nielsen
Salt Lake City, Utah

My Father in His Woodshop

Sawdust shoots onto his bare arms
as he slides the cherry wood
with knotted grain
closer to the blade. It is my birth
he is trying to protect, rather,
a photo of when I was
born. It has been years since
I came home, but if I were
to invent this tableau, I would see
the precision of his method,
how he runs a finger
along the frame, sanding
away the rough edges.
The love he honors by what is done.

I cannot remember if he taught me
how to assemble the pieces
so they lay flush, but
I imagine he did
and that is proof enough.
So to finish the story, because
what remains of memory
exists beyond the last breath,
he will hang it in the foyer,
this one he chose out of many.
He will level the corners
into place, step back to admire
his work, and let loose a grin
like a secret he would never reveal.

Josh Mahler
Centreville, Virginia

Covid-19

My spell checker wants to change
covid to *corvid*, any stout-billed

passerine bird, like a crow or jay or
raven. Or to *coiid*, any member of

an invalid family of fish, now disputed.
Covids have been around awhile, just

not number 19, which no one can figure out:
how it kills (a lot of ways) or

who it chooses (a lot of people).
Fix that, Microsoft Word, because

coved (a sheltered nook) also rids
my page of that shaky red line, as does

caved, which means to fall in,
collapse, give up all opposition to.

Lynda S. Madison
Omaha, Nebraska

hooked

when you sent me the picture of the walleye,
you were honestly proud of yourself and wanted
to share it with someone who appreciates fishing;
the problem is my heart doesn't work that way—
instead, my throat tightens, aches; i imagine i am
getting another chance, which is why i once told you
i am not an ex with whom you can talk because i
will always think a text means you want me back.

let me go.

Gina Marie Bernard
Bemidji, Minnesota

Ark

I see our life together reflected in the surface of a pot
in the curve of a rubber-handled spoon
in the serrated edge of a knife.
Our house is full of metal bits that clatter noisily
as I stomp from one room to another, trying to find purpose
trying to cover up the noise of the other things
that have made their way into our lives:

the dog barking at the mailman dropping packages off at the front door
the daughter jumping and shouting as she follows me through the house
the cat determined to get whatever bits of my attention that are left
the phone that keeps ringing even though we don't know anyone anymore.
I remind myself that some of these things will grow up and move out
the rest will grow old and die, I have become cold and heartless
in my grasping for quiet.

At night, I whisper to you of my dreams of running away
of building a ship out of the fallen birch branches in the back yard
of moving all of my things up to the roof where no one can reach me.
You mutter something in your sleep
it almost sounds like permission
close enough.

Holly Day
Minneapolis, Minnesota

Iowa 80

I speed through Iowa—but not the flyover
        of an airplane's needle stitching all the midwest
                into a Swedish quilt, nor quite as high

as the top of a fast-moving thunderhead
        drumming flat houses, hills and trees,
                the horizon taut enough to snap.

I speed through Iowa—above it, but close enough
        to the earth's curves to lose myself in each valley.
                My lap is a well of sunlight, my eyes blinded blue.

Maybe the only barrier is glass,
        but people become invisible
                inside a semi truck, faces lost

behind bland portmanteaux—Heartland,
        FedEx—and dust settled on the cab door
                like on each of my shoes, gathered

from the couple-hundred steps it takes to cross
        the parking lot of the world's largest truck stop,
                which has served 3 million cups of coffee.

From the truck's cab, Iowa is like a gazing ball,
        a convex world defying logic, 110% more sky
                but also more bald hills, more silver rivers,

more cattle like flies
        scattered in the humid morning—
                a world stretched and filled with itself,

like pregnancy, like a double-reflection
        in a bubble, the heavy strain
                of a droplet about to break.

I speed through Iowa—I can't claim
        to be here, but I am present
                for each rise of the deep-breathing land,

each long mile of meditation.
	Tractor trailers coast the water
		that shimmers across the highway's every dip.

At the Iowa 80, racks of postcards spin
	mobiles of cloud and silo and cow—
		later, from another state, I will post them

out into the world, so that on their way home
	they may pass again through Iowa,
		the journey that is both nothing and too much:

asphalt and air, a super-sized sky,
	the song of eighteen tires, windshield flies,
		moebius horizon, drum of thunder,

Swedish quilts on billboards, a hill
	that births more hills, silo and tree,
		an airplane drawing its cotton thread.

Olivia J. Kiers
Hudson, Massachusetts

Announcement

At first he just stood looking at me
over the hood of his car.
We were parked near the pilings
under the Bay Bridge.
Between the rush of traffic overhead
and the swoosh of wind off the water
he said it,
then quickly turned away
as if trying to deny it
like red tide retreating from the Golden Gate.
Just as quickly he turned back,
reeling out his soul like a fly-fisherman,
to catch up the words,
to swallow them again,
to unspeak.
"*I've got it,*" he said,
"*but I can beat it.*"
It was the way he said it, spirit spraying,
almost abrasive:
he truly believed he could beat it,
swimming upstream like a salmon in heat,
at least he did as he said it.
He didn't say, "*I'm dying,*"
although both of us knew
from that moment on,
he was
the tsunami in motion.

Sam Ambler
Los Angeles, California

Orbits

There have always been rumors about comets:
they cannot hold a steady course,
shed their dust
at the slightest provocation,
and visit other stars
on the sly.
But the comets are fine
and simply living by the truth
that no one chooses the path
that gravity has carved.
We all careen down
our own paths of
least resistance,
every orbit eccentric
from clinging
so hard
to so many
things at once.

Glenn Entis
San Francisco, California

Love of Broken Bodies

We made love with broken bodies
and love was more
than what our broken bodies could hold.

The intricate golden lines of fresco
alive in the silence of a giant cupola,
at the brink of crumbling; for centuries.

Time and space—night and day
were inseparable—we were held
together by dawn and twilight like bichrome frames.

Bold and layered and deep—
our melancholy like a Rothko canvas
suspended between our bodies.

A faint music that has travelled many shores,
has played in spring, blossomed through aeons,
and has grown into the skin of stone.

We reclaimed our selves
from dissipation of a lifetime—
a light in our eyes melted into this truth—here and now.

Madhu Kailas
Thane, India

Witch Hazel (Red Wolf F 1397)

Wolf Conservation Center

Branches in wind, shadows of leaves,
or a shape moving in the thicket?
Figure goes to ground, ground to figure,
a wolf of rusty dirt and clay.
Slender legs, not saplings. Sleek fur,
face all sharp muzzle and pricked ears.

See her head lower, eyes lift, gaze
harden somewhere between pipestone
and liquid amber, and you're fixed,
burning, as if she knew our kind
had hunted hers down to one pack
and she might be safe behind twists
of wire and signs, but she might not.

That tension in shoulders and hips
is fight and flight and lie in wait,
hers and then yours, like a wild scent
rising through your head to send
you out of it, dizzy, aware
you're mortal in every sense.

Dana Sonnenschein
Bethany, Connecticut

Territory

when you grow up in a town like mine,
you learn your measurements early—
how much acreage or mileage you have to spare,
how much room you can account for.

the open fields my grandfather owns spans 103 acres,
and the wooded maze my father shares is 128 acres.

the house that i grew up in sits on the tippy top of a hill,
dead center in the middle of five acres,
about a mile off the highway.

it is exactly 2 thousand, 2 hundred, 17 square feet,
adjusted to exactly 3 hundred 19 thousand, 2 hundred 48 square
    inches,
and i'm sure the allotment of some of it can be accredited to the
    nylon walls
surrounding the exterior,
but it's not like you didn't taint those, too.

if you walked with a pastel pink trail,
i would be the main character
of a kindergarten boy's least beloved book,
where she walks through the bubblegum-colored halls,
into the blush powder room,
then to the strawberry bedroom,
tied together with a pretty pink bow of her magenta pillows.

i think she eats a pink cupcake at the end of the book;
i can't really remember,
i was too focused on the cherry blossom dust you left behind
on every square inch of my house.

maybe the hue made it feel more like a home,
but as the spring pollen set in,
the dust settled into the fibers of my clothes,
and it was washed away with your cologne.

Sara Hebert
Brandon, Mississippi

Seamarks

Those roams of whales
know that below them float
all their ghosts, the living graves

like footprints in clay,
tread studded by bristle
worms, snails, and hooded shrimp.

Or more like tracks in sand. Nothing lasts.
Carcasses dropped across the abyss
a trail, and their trim of shells
shedding tiny teeth will likewise fade away
after the arrows of giants' bones are gone.

What kind of worry could they carry
knowing that another will sink
eventually, a behemoth exhaling
every memory of surface
to take a monument's place.

Sara Wilson
Sidney, British Columbia, Canada

My Daughter Dreams of the Daughter Cut from Her Belly

At three every consonant was H, she sang
Rudolph *had a hairy hinie hose.*

At four she laughed at *hairy hinie.*

Baby clothes, stuffed bears, myriad photos
are both safety net and cage.

My daughter's heart is a reliquary.

In dreams her child is a creeping tiger,
rides a hippo, wears outrageous hats.

She was mother; now she is simply aunt.

The telescope collapses each July—
seven days to encompass a year.

My daughter's heart is a hummingbird.

Fish fly, birds swim, rocks sing.
They discover mysteries together.

Sometimes she takes her hand.

Ann Howells
Carrollton, Texas

Ant Road

There's always a new road to lay,
spraying chemicals on underbrush,
relocating rocks, smoothing on-ramps
flush, prepping the way to dispose
of whatever the hive discards.
Those ants injured or ill who
can't keep up are sent out
along the chute they just built.
We become our own construction,
building insect routes,
rushing someone else's intentions
into reality, climbing ever-higher
stems the better to see what's coming.
We rue any rain that washes away
the scent of safe passage,
we subject (before they flee)
offspring to our tutelage,
we battle what hollows out
tunnels in us even as we tug
the corpse of every day.
Mostly, we obey.

P M F Johnson
Minneapolis, Minnesota

The Robin

Her head bobs like robins' heads do. Bright eyes scan the sky,
which is dense with clouds stacked like books on a shelf,
or wind that has been gathered by wings and left in piles of foam,
the kind of clouds that are possibly the visible evidence of death
pressing its face against the world.

The robin doesn't flee from me. Sure, she bounces awkwardly,
but no flight lifts her wings. As I lean over her,
I see a trail of ants ascending the throne of her ruddy chest.

Ants are busy devouring a leg that barely clings to the robin's body.
Her life is being carried away one molecule at a time,
and she doesn't seem to mind.

I am the only reason for her distress, and as I step back,
she calmly stops wobbling,
teeters briefly on the leg that still belongs to her,
and with patient eyes, returns her attention to the sky.

Hannah Jane Weber
Prairie Village, Kansas

Spinning Class

We pound pedals
with wild determination,
to DJ beats, shouts
of the instructor.

Our limbs glow, center
folds with eyes implying
deeper stories, wheels
humming an angry

script of arguments
we could have started
this afternoon
in the office. Our mist

rises in mirrors,
curated news
to sound-proof clouds.
Soon, as the class ends,

a rainstorm, returning
ache, when we learn
we haven't gone
anywhere.

Gordon Taylor
Toronto, Ontario, Canada

chorus

so many ways
to lose
a queer

everywhere death
is sanctioned, even
sanguine, so,

too, a
lie, a fraud,
can kill

or fantasy, the tyrant
repletion,
a half century's infelicitous

words like so many witness
summons exhausting
sense make sense of

proprioceptive kinesis
in pictures of love
we inherit our inclusion

learn to become our
own accessories out
objects make sub—

queer death
like image death:
ubiquitous, yet holding

—reflexive, in the mourning
a sparkling living
passing murmur—

a rooming house
rented hourly
where hope stays

Jay Buchanan
St. Louis, Missouri

All That Is Left

remorse is a small sad word
uncapitalized, it resides in voices
lost in the dry hollows of bones
and in the dust
when that is all that is left

before the first word
before the first gesture
before the first gasp from the first lung
remorse waited in the dirt

my trail from the womb of the sea
was carved by countless bellies
worn resolutely through centuries of remorse
i followed and did not stop
thinking there must be more ahead—more

and yet, i keep glancing back
to the loveliness of that first nursery
to the buoyancy and taste of salt
to the starlight glinting on waves above me

to the lullabies of my first mother—her seasong
adrift through remorse and the bones of those i've loved
one day she'll sift through the dust of another lost child
when that is all i've come to

Shutta Crum
Ann Arbor, Michigan

Because Tits

Former lover,
You sent me the postcard
sealed tight in envelope.
—*because tits*, you said.
You doubted the sending, and yourself.

You, who made your mother cry
and shake her head "why"
when you told her it was love
and you wouldn't apologize for truth
even when lightning burned through you, and me.

You, thin body stretched
under the weight of a man,
and after, you cradled yourself and said
I'm sorry, and
Never again.

You, Magician-drunk,
stitching petticoat prairie dresses
for the naked queers at the corner-store.
Brown curls—not black—struck through
with silver moon power.

You, tip-toe on the highest ladder rung,
brightening office walls with purple.
Walls that shiver with tales
heard from quivering mouths and
purple-bruised faces.

You sealed her (us) up in envelope,
Because we never stopped hearing Valenzuela's voice;
we Juan-and-Mariana-ed our love,
stamped our envelopes with kisses,
feared our exchanges for who might see them.

My lover,
You never left my skin.
I taste lavender as I read you in.
I cry, and shake my head "why"
—*because tits*—the world says.

Paige M. Ferro
Bend, Oregon

Pour Water on Me

She was at one of the windows,
in a wheel chair—this woman
I didn't know—her face
right up to the window,
almost touching.
Heavy maroon drapes
framed each window—
framed her—
framed the enactment.
Her focus
just outside the window
into a courtyard.

Her utterances
were like weeping,
and she did weep
quietly
and she spoke,
You are so beautiful.
Why don't you come in.
Please come in
and pour
water on me.

I heard it
as I passed behind her
on the way to find
my mother.
The woman at the window,
a constant stream of moaning
and whimpers
asking the one
outside—
where there was no one—
to come in
to her.

My mother
speaks rarely
and in broken bits.
She performs
actions—
shelling peas, I think,
and putting something
pot to pot. Often
she works the seams
of my clothes
like she was fitting
a dress to me,
the dress wrong-side-out,
and she had pinned
the seams
where she would sew.
Now tugging at my clothes,
arguing with what I wore that day,
wanting the shoulder seams
to rest
in a different place.

One day
my mother
was pouring
something.
She lifted
the unseen
vessel—
tilting it,
pouring.
I wanted to catch the liquid
in my hands,
bend over
put my head
under the spout,
feel
this stream
she drained
from her

pitcher.
I wanted it to flow
over me,
what she poured
into the air
invisible
as the scrim
its loose folds
encircling us.

Jeannie Gambill
Bellaire, Texas

inferno

i grew up on the corner of
bittersweet and melancholy
our house made of matchsticks
painted robins egg blue
to disguise our precarious life
built from kindling

my brother was a spark
and it wasn't until
they brought me home
and he and i mixed
that they first found out
i was gasoline

we stayed in the house on fire
choking on smoke
through fake smiles
laughing about the heat
and telling ourselves
we were phoenix like

i wish i could grow up
move away from home
past bittersweet and melancholy
out of decay and destruction
wash cinder from my body
for the last time

but how can i become anything
be reborn from the ash
when all that is left of me
when my brother was through
are wisps of smoke
in the shape of a girl

Charlie Quayle
Astoria, New York

Snow, Frost, Moon

I get up from the bed
in nothing but my knee socks
and my sex hair, to go stand
at the frosted window pane,
not caring who sees me or if
I catch my death with the sweat
drying to my body. I crack it a bit
and rest my cheek against the ledge,
gulping the icy air, not caring
if anyone knows that we've been
seeking the heat of each other's
cavities, that we've been tied
together in a knot of blankets and
flannel sheets. The nape of my neck
damp, my upper lip glistening
like new snow. Globular December
moon: jizz-white on a black quilt,
celestial money shot pearling
midnight's tits. First, I had to
get warm. Now, I have to
get cold again. How else
will I dive back into bed with you,
how else can I don your skin again?
You could take a handful of snow
and dribble it on my steaming
body, split me open. Season of craving,
that brings to the fore our lust
for salt and fat, for heaviness,
for honey-thick fluids,
for stick-to-your-ribs satisfaction.
I fall back against you and melt
all over the bedding. Outside,
tree branches creak and groan
beneath the weight of their
winter burden, as the mattress
creaks and groans beneath
the weight of us. We must not
waste these long nights.

Silver dawn will find the thrash
of the snow angels we've left behind.

Lauren Scharhag
Kansas City, Missouri

V838 of Monoceros

She's in love with fire.
She is fire.
But her house is so small.

There was a time when
she'd finally had enough.
She raged in the night,
burned her red dress,
her star crown. Sent a
fire shout across the
sleeping universe.

If you ask,
she won't remember
what brought it on,
just that it was delicious
to destroy a little bit
of all that dark.

Hubble noted the mood
had changed in her finite
constellation, and watched
helplessly

as she incinerated,
thrummed her body
into a torch so bright,
the scar
still bleeds.

Carolyn Adams
Beaverton, Oregon

Pollen

One day we will be
light,
weightless as pollen,
scattered without
even the wealth of shadows.
We will see then
how shallow our river
of breath ran, how
we barely filled ourselves
with the rollicking sky, the way
a glove fills with the warmth of hands,
expands, gives in
to the push, pull of fingers,
merging within &
without, no longer almost,
but there, symbiotic as root & leaf,
seamless & we,
suddenly ancient, with
too much in common with the last few
rustling leaves whipped in
wind & we
will move through
mist,
like wolves dreamed,   at dawn,
move through falling
snow,
leaving tracks.   If you would care to
see.

Rose Maria Woodson
Oak Park, Illinois

Aubade

I know it is just physics—that light
scattering through atmosphere
is the reason for this display,
but I can't help but think
there is something more to it
that calls us to speak and try to soothe
this terrible ache to connect.

Don't we all wish we were painters
so we could capture what rises before us—
the myriad reds, electric-blue windows,
the silver curve of the elevated train
before it plunges into the earth?

Words break down before this splendor.
You do not see what I see;
yet I believe we can meet somehow
each beginning and ending our day
in beauty even though separated
by this broken expanse of white.

Ivana Mestrovic
Long Island City, New York

Plowing

Should have stayed with us the kin said.
Should not have walked the lame horse

from the barn to the field. Though I wonder
if the lame horse knew the cutoff point.

How far into the field before the farmer
shot what he thought to be the horse,

only to have the bullet hit the fence post,
and how after, the farmer begged the horse

to plow, plow through the deep furrow
of time, memory. Neighing, the horse

scratched the earth, not sure if the farmer
saw the scarecrow at the turn off row,

the scarecrow eager, eager to try on
the farmer's hat, coat. For the farmer's

time had been plowed under, deep
into the earth. How the farmer rode

death, a wild horse, back to the barn.
How the lame horse never caught up.

Mary Ann Meade
Lansdowne, Pennsylvania

My Daughter, Practicing the Cello

Sound slithers out
from under the closed door
to her teenage bedroom
as she winds her way slowly
up the serpentine spiral
of a scale, her horsehair bow
drawing long notes out
of the instrument the way
a snake charmer's flute
uncoils a length of cobra
from a woven basket,
coaxing it out bit by bit
and then easing it back
down the way it came. In
and out of keys she glides,
ascending and descending
and, ultimately, distilling
the oft-venomous world
of an adolescent down into
an orderly series of notes,
something she can exercise
some control over and,
in time, even tame.

Michael Hill
Fort Collins, Colorado

Starfish

I lose a dimension every time someone leaves,
and someone is always leaving.

This is my fault, as I have been warned by someone
who knows things that people, like starfish,

don't last, being made of fragile and improbable things,
like tessellations and raspberry jam.

In other news, I still have six basil plants in the window,
which puts us at a 25% survival rate.

This, I have found, is normal not only for basil,
but for life in general.

Most of the things I care about other than basil
are stranded in tide pools

which means they have three to five minutes to live,
once the tidepools dry up.

I wish someone had told me it was about to get so
unfunny. I might have prepared

myself better, steeled my senses against the salt smell
of death by open air.

Soon I will be a single point in space, a singularity
taking up no room.

From here I will be able to see the dust glowing
in the streets of outer space.

The basil growing
at the bottom of the sea.

Shannon Lise
Québec, QC, Canada

Certainty

Something calls from the holler,
calls again in the brushed silence
of sun-glossed autumn leaves.
Almost a shrieking, not quite
a caw or scream, sound of metal
tearing, vocalized and spit back
through a beak's hollow portent,
so, it must be a bird of sorts.
But the spot of a red-tailed hawk
circling just below the cloud-mist
is too high up, too certain
in its fixed circumference of sky
to have possibly made the call.
Perhaps the sound, the shrieking,
was meant to summon the one
above—a mate calling, or neighbor
warning, *this space in the holler
is occupied.* As if in answer
a train whistle lows, borrowing
distance. The steady rumble
of the rail's steel wheelsets
is another destination to reach
mile after mile away. Another
ending that cannot be heard—
the holler stills, the call goes
silent, everything imperceptible
waits for the coming cold.

Timothy Geiger
Swanton, Ohio

Because I'm Thirty-Five and Not Fifteen

after Sandra Cisneros

I haven't written
a suicide poem
since I was a teenager
and I'm not gonna
break my streak

but goddamn.

I'm every day crying
and the children
are every day crying
and my wife
is every day crying

and it never stops.

The islands where
I once lived, happy,
fenced out this plague
but I'm stranded here
in this shithole country

and I can't leave.

But I'm not gonna
write that poem.

Holly Painter
South Burlington, Vermont

Poets Exploiting Real Trees for Their Metaphors

There was talk about trees among the poets
who I thought had long ago used up brambles and branches to
    insinuate the tangles
of family connections, their senescing leaves spelling seasons of
    decline,
the downfall of dynasties, and their trunks, of course, standing for
    fortitude,

so when the talk finally got around to unbridled lumbering and
    dying rainforests
the walnut tree in Jessie's yard came to mind,
its cooling shade more generous than Longfellow's chestnut tree.
In spite of its annual litter, I loved its sway, what sang and nested in
    its mazes.

Something besides birds showed up, burrowed in, and the tree
    thinned.
Bits of bark began peeling, I'd hear twigs cracking off in the night,
brittle limbs letting the wind take them, snow taking them down in
    winter.
The yard began to change, like a peach skin withering at its soft spot.

So much the poets took from trees, from Blake to Lorca to Frost,
from Frost's swinger of birches to Lorca's *arbolés*, to Yeats, who wrote
    of the holy trees
in the heart, and the Garden's trees, and the Sephirotic Tree of Life
    stretching to heaven,
yet firmly stuck in earth. They left the stump.

Looking now across Jessie's lawn, I can see clear to the back fence,
pear trees once obscured. The leafy play of sun gone, there's a starker
    sense of tenure.
So I steal a line from Yeats, not one about trees, but words that
    uncover.
A terrible beauty is born. A body after fever. The woods after fire.

Florence Weinberger
Malibu, California

Haystacks

It takes a day to make a haystack.
It takes three workers working all day—
one to move the hay from windrows,
two to stack. There's an art to the making—
getting stems to interleave in such a way
they make rounded stacks that shed
rain and snow. An interleaving of form
and purpose although I doubt the haystack
makers think of it that way.

They may not think at all but feel—the weight
of fork in hand, the weight of sun by afternoon
as one levers hay to the one who builds
the layers of the stack, its width and height by feel.
These forms that rise in fields prove that fields
are never empty. The hay has use. The grass
comes back green in spring.

Mark Simpson
Clinton, Washington

Dominoes

It's your birthday, and I have no idea
where you are—but I'm told it's heaven
or somewhere close by. The years have not
cleared up anything for me, and life hasn't
let up. Clouds remain swollen.

Hanging with grief is not for the weak—
and you lose some friends along with way.
The days fall like dominoes. Long walks,
no answers; the sky on high alert. It gets
easier, but never easy.

Stay positive. Stay calm. Stay clean, stay sober.
Stay hopeful. Just stay—as if slogans
can slow the roll.

And I can't remember why we disagreed
on the validity of ghosts—as if we had
all the time in the universe to kick up dust.

But it's your birthday; it doesn't matter
where you are. You can hang with anyone
and fit right in.

Cathy Porter
Omaha, Nebraska

Shelter

A friend braces himself on waking every morning
for police to knock on his door
to say his son is dead.

Attempted rescue over years, rehabilitation
in different states, offers of compromise life
unaccepted.

This, he feels, is rage
expressed in dying.

He places photographs of the child,
the youth, young man on his mantel.

Talks to people at the homeless shelter
in that far city, who have seen him,
but won't share information,
and a cop who takes his calls, who told him,
This is the final spiral of terminal addiction.

He reads stories about the lives of street addicts
to hold his son inside.

Our new puppy, on her fifth day here, presses against us,
sleeps on our feet as we stand talking,
chews on a toy, head on my leg
looking up at me with her blue brown eyes.

Joseph Hardy
Nashville, Tennessee

A Spectacular Blessing at St. Francis

A coffee splatters in Cardiac Registration
over the tile floor, and all the pasty
haunted faces turn

to watch the spiller bee-swatting
her sweatshirt and sweatpants, muddy
puddles spreading. *Spill!*

Cardiac Registration!, the fluttering receptionist
calls to *Environmental Services*, cautions
all in her tense-ish, calm-ish pitch.

Careful, Love, squeezing a shoulder, *Slippery,
Dear,* pats a hand. And for a few unmonitored
heartbeats, some unconsidered

inhales and exhales—the shock
of recent worst-case diagnoses confirmed,
the calculating and recalculating of risks—anesthesia,

surgery, postponement, pain
and then what, and then what—vanish
as the woman in khaki scrubs rolls

in her yellow bucket
and with steady, sweeping swabs,
works her mop.

Michael Mark
San Diego, California

body heat

infrared homing is a passive weapon guidance
system which uses infrared light emission from
a target to track it and follow it. it. it. what is
my guidance system? what is my target? what
is heat? what is fever? where does fever start?
what kind of light do i emit? the obverse is
time; the time is now. it's always now. the time
has always already passed you by. it's always
just on the verge of novel magic, of drawing
blood, like an arrow seeks its deer or like the
world's first train: we only need to lay the tracks
out before us. the walls spin & mix together but
of course they do. they are made of paint.
missiles which use infrared seeking are
often referred to as "heat-seekers," since
infrared is radiated strongly by hot bodies,
many objects such as people but how can i
say what i mean? each word is hideous
to me. in the heat of the moment (i'm sorry)
i said i was a deer. i lied. i am a man.
this is not my first or second winter.
i was born in a snowstorm. i told you
all about it. i was there.

Patrick Younger
Kansas City, Missouri

A Portrait of My Father as a Young Waif

Against a schoolroom chalkboard,
rumpled, hair awry, he has a look
of being in a twilight in a world
where his latch-key doesn't fit.

      "I dug and dug amongst the snow
        And thought the flowers would never grow,"
it says in someone's inspirational hand
on the board behind the children.

Depression circles in the sky;
so many things are incubating.
And Hardship never reads the papers
or reflects on causes or effects.

Father's world is an old clock
and the key to wind it is lost.
The weather on the way to school
is boom or bust; he's become

the boy in Dickens with a broom
who sweeps the street crossing
for a rich man's carriage.
It is his desire to be that man

that keeps him there, feet cold,
at the side of another's road.
Like the others he has the look
of the snowblind in a blizzard.

Their eyes are the keys that don't
fit; the future's a snowbound road.
The expressions say nothing of what
the teachers taught that day

and my father, an aged child
like the rest, has what would be
a hundred year old face
that shows the effects of seasons

of seeking flowers in the snow.

Todd Johnson
Racine, Wisconsin

Shadows

walk slough-side
near train tracks
through foxglove and brambles
as the sun sets on Prairie Market
and the phone booth at Dairy Queen
freeway ramp and driveway gravel
rotting apples
lawn chairs
back door
and kitchen
where night comes early
to the curtainless window
amid ghosts of freight from Black River Junction
steamboat wheels tangled in reeds

Samantha Malay
Seattle, Washington

How we must recognize this place

Rain tattoos a rhythm on the
      sagging blue tarp that covers our tent.
It is anchored but tenuously to the earth,
As we are also,
Cleaved to each other
Like stakes wedged in rocky soil.

Wind threatens, but the tarp holds.
We lie back, eyes lifted
      to our sheltered sky,
Breathing in the ever-present damp mossness
      of this place,
Bound already to its rushing tides
      and heaving waters,

Fixed to each other
Through the wind,
The water,
The waves.
Marooned here.

Fog slithers up the hill, across the Bay of Fundy
On the bank opposite where we are hunkered down,
Fingerlike tendrils seeking seals as they bask on the rocks,
      away from the creeping tide.

We know weather is coming when the chittering squirrels
      fall silent,
The foghorn at Cape Spencer booms,
And the crows settle in treetops with a murmur
Like purring through marbles in their throats.

Suzannah Kolbeck
Baltimore, Maryland

Lures

a fishy eye
shines
with peril
the silver sea
pants
against bare feet
a song
slithers
like a hook
among rocks
jaws of siren
glisten
sweet
and they keep coming
one after another
Eve
and her apple
wisecracks

Hollie Dugas
Las Cruces, New Mexico

KwickAssess

With KwickAssess, you'll do much less,
eliminate the need to guess
about a work of art, a mate,
an applicant, a candidate.
Our algorithm takes the stress

of choice away. So why obsess?
Adjust the software to address
hardware beliefs, remove debate.
With KwickAssess, you'll do much less!

Or click for KwickAssessExpress.
Side effects include gray matter loss
of self-reliance catatonic state
The diamond upgrade now! Don't wait!
The fastest pathway to success—
Do less—with KwickAssessExpress!

Diane Thiel
Albuquerque, New Mexico

Taste Will Die with Us

The sky, bleached of rage, settles
in gray, a dollhouse mirror.

Don't look inside warns the shopkeeps
whose windows resist peeping, immaculately

chrome so the eye can
never adjust. Here,

our kitchen sinks rust in symbolism
& you can, for a *low, low price!*

find an interpreter—interpretation
is not a scammer's market,

though you should be
wary of too many positives.

Most spend themselves
at the pool house, where

extensive measures have been taken
to replicate the old sky's rosy

undertones. The water, I can assure you,
is sterile, like us. We are of the few

who tried gutting
ourselves, but babies

always find a way in a vacuum.
So, we sterilized the water

& the water sterilizes—
the last mutual symbiosis. Tonight

is ladies' night. All fourteen of us,
chemically dried, bobbing

in stinging stagnancy, the pool
house's army of Poseidon

statues overseeing our aerobics. We
flutter kick & splash

flirtatious, gentle lapping
at Poseidons' feet. This is our only

indulgence but when we prune, our ethic
loosens & we spiral beneath

the Poseidons, mouths open.
At home, our sinks rust in vulgar

arrangements. We wade, waiting
for one of us to snap from trance & ask

*Why would the statue be anything
else?* We slink back to the locker rooms,

lick the chlorine from each other's faces—
it's best to sterilize taste, too.

Taste is desire that won't
surrender. We can

overcome the drive to fill
our homes but not ourselves.

The bleached sky offers no
gradation, its night shift too

sudden for the eye
to catch. But it's possible

we've just forgotten
how to look for these things.

Rachel Stempel
New Hyde Park, New York

Worm Farm

1.

I'd sure like to buy us a worm farm
for all our lemon rind needs,

for all those avocado pits that skip
across the countertop like oaken marbles

the size of squash balls, slick
with oil-green meat. I'd love to see

how you'd let it all rot, properly rot, into
something serviceable & neat. You'd rear

the worms so skillfully, peering in
to see their pink-gray bodies,

writhing in earth-ecstasy, throng
the plastic structure where they'd weep

at first to find themselves alive. Driving five
minutes late to your first guitar lesson I say babe

let's spring for the Vermihut Pro, let's raise
those little suckers up all grotesque

& inevitable and after a pause
you say, and I quote, *why though*—

you've heard the good ones
come steep, and when it works

which it never does, it reeks
like shit. Usually they just die in there

or you break up and someone cares
for them alone, regretting it. I park,

you strap on your N-95 & leave to learn
the A-minor chord then forget it. I sit in the car.

2.

They say when the pit slips out
it's light, lighter than expected:

almost hollow, the avocado losing
so little in losing this, its center.

I won't get emotional. It's not
a baby, and there is no baby, and there

won't be. But when I extract
the sticky ball from its livid hole

and put it in the little compost bin
I settled for, I wish the knife would lift me

into the pain I'll never have to twist
through, or at least open me up

a little more. Courtney making guacamole once
mentioned in passing the recommended method

for extracting the pit had backfired;
a mis-angled whack split open her left hand

& sent her to the ER in Philly, the long wait
just time enough to laugh. She's a mother now

like everyone—I'm not even sure
whether it's a girl. Only some worm breeds

could have digested that avocado pit
stained with Courtney's blood. "The red wigglers

love it!" exclaims the author of dengarden.com
but the comments aren't so sure—

like me most worms are vegetarians,
a trait I treasure in them more and more.

They burrow in the question of a love,
surfacing only when, plugging the nose

and wearing gloves, one tries to pry ajar
the worm farm's latch-style door.

Hannah Loeb
Charlottesville, Virginia

In the Weeds

Call the plant by its homeliest name—
Goutweed, not Snow on the Mountain
Nor *Ameo Bastardo* nor yet Bishop's Weed.
This pernicious smotherer of other plants
Requires concrete restraints to control its spread.

An afternoon spent untangling meaning from
Bishop's "Weed" leaves my vision blurred,
My mind too muddy to respond to a setting sun
Slanting though the sliding glass door and across
The pages. My mind melts, a pool of misery.

Bless the rumored power of the weed's aromatic seeds
To treat psoriasis, asthma, angina, even kidney stones.
Beware side effects. Call it hepatoxin. Or anticoagulant.
Risk sun sensitivity. Swallow the bitter tisane. Overcome
Lassitude, as insidious as any crawling root.

Do I understand it all? This allegory, this surreal landscape?
This plant will not be poisoned. These rivers will not
Be dammed. Though they meet the heart's division
With dread, dreamers will come to welcome drops of water
Swollen with illuminations of each scene the rivers engulfed.

Trina Gaynon
Beaverton, Oregon

Embrace

My neighbour, an upright man,
who feeds the hood's kittens twice a day,
rises with the sun along fresh, slim slopes
curling about sunflower boxes;
toddlers, climbing up to school with their eyelids low,
mittened hands wrapped in their parents', chilled by the late
    autumn—
brighten like little moons, run to my neighbour,
and put their arms around his knees.
These kids must have been really wanted,
I thought.

Dripping, my tiny pinewood desk,
chipped in all directions,
with oil. Mother used to quaff her beer
and knock the candles off around my bunk.
After her, I have always sought out
houses on fire
to embrace.

Amelia Sitou
Geneva, Switzerland

Settled

I don't know why I float but I float.
Don't reason breathing but take
the weight it offers and its

lightness. Where did the cold place go?
Maybe it burned down, who knows,
not me. In childhood, the giants.

We knew they were coming.
Later, stepping through sirens.
Now the jingle of the rabies tag

in the night has me sitting up going
what? hello? No need to ask why I love,
or you. Proof's the fact we float. We float.

Nancy White
Cambridge, New York

Exercise

There was, like lots of them usually
say, a way to go, in what many
like to call—The Journey—with, you know,
how they like to capitalize both
a big T and J, but we were there
on the road to somewhere when we
came to a fork in the road at a bad
time, like on a dark and stormy day
or some other cliché that we like
to grab onto as some sort of life
preserver, like if we were suddenly lost
at sea in a metaphor, when we had
been, really really really, like only
standing on a dry strand of dark dirt
next to a car with a really flat tire
out beside those parallax corn rows
where you know the lines between
the fixed rows keep on hypnotically
shifting shifting shifting but always
stay staying the same geometrically but
of course they'd stopped shifting because
with a flat the car stopped moving
down the strange road we didn't know
because we took the fork least traveled
and wound up here where we are, lost
again strictly in metaphor at sea

Michael J. Shepley
Sacramento, California

Double Header Duet

for Irene

I picture you seated in the crowd, waiting for an
Omaha Storm Chasers baseball game to begin.
You sit in solid stadium seats,
Your feet propped up on the empty seat in front,
You hold a copy of Patchett's *Bel Canto,*
(A finger marks your place)
Ready to be read between innings.
Wearing shorts and a College World Series t-shirt,
Your glasses catch light from the sun,
You turn to the couple beside you, tell them of
Your admiration of the soprano's aria,
Performed at the opera you attended last week.

I picture you seated in the audience, waiting for an
Opera Omaha performance of Madam Butterfly to begin.
You sit in plush theater seats,
Your feet tucked back under out of the way,
You hold a copy of Boswell's *Why Time Begins on Opening Day,*
(A finger marks your place)
Ready to be read during intermission.
Wearing a classic attending-the-arts black dress,
Your glasses catch light from the stage,
You turn to the couple beside you, tell them of
Your admiration of the outfielder's catch,
Made in the baseball game you attended last week.

Margo L. Foreman
Lincoln, Nebraska

Evangeline Throughway

after "Equilibrium" by Tiana Clark

Three women padding in bare feet around the
wood floors of a clapboard home amidst the flat
flat wasteland of Louisiana lawns
Three generations— mother, daughter and
grandmother split open wide with grief
and joy, finding comfort in each
other's laughter during this
forbidden corona virus visit
Been forty years since I lived here
a neighborhood cut in two by a three-lane
throughway tearing the breastbone apart
with an asphalt cleaver leveling the
once sleepy quiet dead-end road with
a highway of noise and speed and rage
An onslaught of upward mobility, a
race to the malls, and I-10, endless yellow
broken-line consumerism and hollow
progress for some. What persists is
a thick coat of endless black soot and dirt
the filth of a capitalist nation high on
trampling over, plowing under, and obliterating
the communities of those lacking power
money, or white faces. So cut me open and
watch me bleed, splay me down the
middle as my neighborhood loses their jobs, their
homes, their respect and then shake your
head and proclaim Such a shame!
That used to be such a "nice" neighborhood
and now look at it— all boarded up houses
dirt yards, nowhere to shop, not even a 7-11
and so much crime. We few survive
as a family no matter the
scars we carry

Nicole Farmer
Asheville, North Carolina

Lessons

I want to run backwards
Through time
To find the 14-year-old me,
To define what words
Like predator mean.
I don't want to learn
The hard way anymore;
I wish I had never learned at all
What it means for a man
To stand over me, smirk pulled
Back tight against his gums,
A full eight feet tall—
I wish I didn't know what fear
Tasted like, but more so I wish
I didn't know what his hands
Tasted like as they shoved their way
Behind my teeth, showing me
That I can still be "sexy"
Even while he's raping me.
There is still a part of me
Digging through thesauruses
In the back of my mind, trying
And miserably failing to define
This gaping hole between my thighs;
I'm still searching for a definition,
A reasoning, a more fitting word
Than "grooming," but most of all
I am desperate to find a way
To report a robbery
Of all the pieces inside of me.

Maggie Bowyer
Greensboro, North Carolina

The Folks in 1921

had the benefit of lively barbers
and straight blades, fresh eggs
and Teddy bears, Babe Ruth
and awful mastodons going up
at museums across the nation.
Their mornings mostly noiseless,
they read the local news and bled
in private.

My grandmother
went in search of black ribbons
for her hair, the kind the older girls
wore, and bracelets for her arms.
For her, the War meant a myth
concluded, so she danced
to songs no one recognized:
Eddie Cantor's "Margie"

and the "Wang Wang Blues."
To be alive meant kegs of beer
and a Model T Ford. For her, the boy
that drove one seemed a god
undeterred. I imagine her—
as in that Williams poem—clutching
a flower

of cotton candy and asking why
the Catholic boys on South Pardee
were more handsome
than her cousins. Her demands
all cloaked as questions,
she was the true,

more American than I
and stronger than you. Years later,
when the nothing came
inside her days, she found nickels
in her shoes and turned them
into soup and dollars.

Carl Boon
Barberton, Ohio

Attar of Alfalfa

Potent as a barber's aftershave,
the aroma of alfalfa followed
my father throughout its days
of bloom, through his mowing,
raking, stacking, an aroma
pure and purple pouring
from the zillion blossoms
blanketing the hill,
flitting forth with butterflies
and drifting on the wind,
then on cold days
of the winter, how
the cattle must have
savored that purple
fragrance salted deep
inside their breakfast hay.

Marilyn Dorf
Lincoln, Nebraska

I Was Blessed by Two Lovely Lil' Sprites, I Was.

A red-headed, green-eyed mermaid
slipped too early out the door,
dropping into the waters creating
ripples to break silently on the far shore
like the tear drops that fell beside her.

Her sister a blonde, blue-eyed fairy,
kept her wings hidden 'til she was grown.
But she danced from sun-up to sun-down
flitting from one thing to the next
with the grace of a butterfly.

Weavers, they were, my darlings.
The fairy making a path upward
ducking her head at low blows
and clambering over obstacles.

While the mermaid undulated
through rough and tumble rivers,
dipping and leaping on her way
to the sea she'd call home.

All the while their heart strings
tugging at me to turn them loose.

Charlene Neely
Lincoln, Nebraska

Truancy

She said she knew something about leaving
the weight curling in your bones
and refusing exit.

She said she made that mistake once
when she named two cats she knew
were not hers; were "nobody else's really,
but definitely not mine."

They hissed at her, white snakes in anger,
claws ready to grow inward.

She left them before
"They bit their white out,"
like what you love
can despise itself.

She said she nearly broke down
Again
When they gave her a plastic pink whistle
the kind that had a bell in it
that rattles every time you breathe.
the kind chewed down with use
the kind that lodges itself in gaps
and never returns.

The kind that you give to miscreant children
with which they scream-whistle
"I'm still here, I'm still here."
as they sink into the night,
purpled with slipshod suns.

When she heard of those birds in Manipur
who come October,
dive into flames
"for no fathomable reason:
reverse phoenixes"
She said she gasped,
"Heart, my heart, this, my heart."

Meaning *jigar*, meaning liver, meaning easily torn apart meaning
so so so precious
meaning gone.

Stuti Pachisia
Cambridge, United Kingdom

Another Piece of Music

My mother loved classical music.
> We left the radio on by the hospital bed and barely knew
> what played.

Debussy sometimes, though she favored opera.

Music made us feel better about leaving her downstairs at night,
> comatose.

The Somali aide we hired was too terrified
to be left alone with Mom's soft breathing,
lest her soul
> creep out
> > like mist lifting off the day—strangely savage—

to confront the sentinel at the witching hour.

The aide cowered obediently
till I went up to bed,
when she bolted into our bright kitchen
to Beethoven's Third.

Sorry, Mom!

I was with her during the day—
"Moonlight Sonata" at night—

I set the alarm to turn her
every three hours or so.

I medicated her as she slept at death's doorway.
I waited and watched for her last rattle.
Ravel's *Boléro*?

Morphine at the end, good night, "Clair de Lune."

The radio played on without her.

Laura Celise Lippman
Seattle, Washington

Aruncus Dioicus

Of a spring-gift sundown, splashed in coquelicot,
near where, time out of mind, egrets in pairing

have hatched and plumbed and, clambering the stone-
wrought ruins of a relic cottage hearth, rise wild

Souvenirs de la Malmaison, the tea scent gush
a profusion overspreading both he and she until

enchantment leashes their listening to wonder—

of such a gift, in this old marshland consecrate
to mysteries, upon a bed of budding shoots

(goat's beard some call them, puffed as lechery against
their skin as they roil together, slowly, madly,

devoutly impudent, creamy plumes above veiny
toothy leaflets—bride's feathers, others say)

in the dwindling, they clutch as night descends.

Greg Sendi
Chicago, Illinois

Police Report

A car strikes
a disabled woman in a motorized wheelchair
who crosses at Park Lake and 19th.
An ambulance takes her to the hospital.
It was sudden impulse, she says,
like an unexpected storm,
or a flood when the ice breaks.
She wheels to her nearby apartment
after grocery shopping.
The police say she throws her wheelchair in gear
to cross Park Lake Drive in heavy traffic
when the light is about to turn red.
A Mitsubishi Eclipse heads south on North 19th.
Another vehicle blocks
the driver's view of the wheelchair.
The car knocks her from her wheelchair
onto the pavement
with a cry about her groceries.
Then she is taken to the hospital.
She is treated for scratches and bruises.
The police gather up her groceries.
They warn her several times
about the wheelchair in the middle of the road.
She says there are so many breaks and short ends
in life,
nothing can be spun into an even piece.
She cries she broke some sort of Sabbath
and that her tuna tin is missing.

J. Alan Nelson
Waco, Texas

Revelation

I found horror in a fistful of pale ash,
dreams mangled along nine rows of crooked teeth
where seven devils danced to empty howls
between hollows of orange trees.

Their eyes—milky and glass,
speaking without tongues:
why is the night the color of rust?

A finch, a lark, and one grey fox linger
beneath the singed earth
the brined dirt
feasting memory as meat
drinking in memorial
of how the meek will inherit
all we walk upon
      —all this dust.

The mind unveils,
transmutes silver into amalgam
vision glows faintly in crosses and circles,
      —bound in bone, in membrane.

Mark Burr
Ocean Springs, Mississippi

Bishop's Wort

every April pokes its head
        up through
the tight-lipped congregation,

shoulders aside pachysandra,
        petit point lace
umbels lifted in some

silent benediction,

each knot of pistil / stamen
        fist of one more
pale pilgrim offering flowers

barely worth a nod until
        we count
the vanishingly tiny

    seeds.

Bill Griffin
Elkin, North Carolina

World in Motion

My daughter, frantic in the midnight, wakes me to drive her,
holds the texted suicide note phone in her hand.

In the ER waiting room, the father cries, tells how he had tried
to hold her up, call 911. He curses the boyfriend who'd broken
up with her from the Army by text, threatens to kill him.

The divorced parents talk of their daughter's manic-depression—
maybe she'd be luckier not to live.

My yellow hoodie shrouds my face somewhat protects
my neck from hospital cold as stress clenches every muscle.

The thin hand on the Pegasus clock ticks 360 degrees,
a mechanical pulse measuring seconds as the night creeps by.

A van pulls up to the ER drop off. A man hops out, leaving
the door gaping. He runs through the ER doors, returns
to the passenger side with a wheelchair, rushes his laboring wife
past as a nurse instructs: take that elevator to the maternity wing.

By the security office door sits a box labeled "human organs."
Printed on the side are icons for body parts—one of them eyes.

We wait hours for a specialist. My daughter sits in the parking lot
with the other best friend she hadn't seen earlier that night.

A pair of rabbits frolics on the lawn near the hospital entrance.

The specialist comes and goes. My daughter and her friend trail
a nurse through ER doors, are allowed to say good-bye before—

The dark granite boulder at the visitor entrance is meant to revolve
when water flows beneath it. As the morning shift arrives,
a custodian turns on the water, setting the world in motion.

Jeanne Blum Lesinski
Saginaw, Michigan

Before You Return to Civilization

minor roads, slow hills, a poet's prose from some western
moors of Wyoming—cloud drift, salt shores in black coal
charcoal drawing chill

ice remember, frost forget as city friends force in their
heater warmth. you sit again as a citizen of the town,
respected, placed—happily, happy this time
away from the dance of the wind, coyote trail to nowhere

but this is not to be wasted, you know, come passion, come
passions caught in the high plains these seasons of snow

a prairie myth: to button a coat and become too warm

and a lesser story, still vivid, of the movement from
rocket arctic air to the breathless metallic of a frosted car
the soul-still house

soul-still and bone bare, the prairie strips
care, passion for the blood of love as you
hammer stub feet on the rock freeze, the prairie empty
cold and yet you care, tongue numb

in civilization to try again

this is not to be wasted, you know

these slow hills of seasons change
and change

cold hands, cold feet, and love

Elaine Verdill
Windsor, Colorado

Hyphens

When she was born, her father refused to hold her.
He said he was afraid he would break her.
As her cradle swayed, she wondered:
Was she made of glass?
Were her pretzel-like fingers too fragile to wrap around his thumb?
She got older,
and in steam-cloaked shower doors,
and in fog-padded car windows,
her bitter fingers sway to paint questions like: why? and
what-did-I-ever-do-to-you?
A woman stands in a corner
and silently thinks about the world.
The one before. The one to come.
An old Arabic saying rings:
When a thing is feared, it turns up at every corner.
Hyphens are bridges,
and periods are deadly shots that cut off circulation.
She looks back. She looks ahead.
Faint words make their way into her eye:
Your honesty is going to destroy you, dear—
minus the "dear"—
of course.

Shurouq Ibrahim
Dublin, Ohio

Work Days*

Four details under command,
sentries posted and hidden
near fellers, haulers and carpenters,
protecting the wattling men.

Trees slash through breezes,
the branches trimmed, and begun
in warmth of breath with a gill
poured now-and-again.

Those who favor chunking wood
possess their hand-hewn tools
that constant motion wears to smooth.
The lazy ones act the fools.

With hide buckets full of mud,
leaves and twigs for wattle,
one man inside, one made out,
both chinking on one bottle.

Logs are notched and placed.
An ox does shake its coat,
our goods and blankets drying out
as Floyd tallies up the Boat.

Willard and Roberson have returned
with letters from St. Louis,
news of streets and wooden walks
and women sightings to remind us.

They help to stow heavy stores
in good order, then amuse us all
with stories of excess to please us,
stretching them up real tall.

Ice builds. We caulk and trim.
Whitehouse and York apace,
two sawyers with a saw that sings
back and forth in place.

Winds do give, then take away
that bee-sweet scent of resin;
from seasoned arms a tug-of-war
between them both can win.

Repeating a task is never easy,
to relax the strength until
the calming frees a bind—a pace
is best that ends in skill.

Mark B. Hamilton
Dunedin, Florida

*History-based verse, adapted from "Wintering at Camp Dubois," Vol.
2, *The Journals of the Lewis & Clark Expedition*, Gary E. Moulton, editor.
Lincoln: University of Nebraska Press, 1986.

Restraint

On this stretch of street
flanked by yards
of boredom
yawning wide—
every blade
stands straight
as an Eisenhower
era haircut.
Through stay-at-home
orders or quarantines,
these lawns tended
with the detail of bonsai
or a seafoam kitchen—
the gaps between slabs
and cobble teased clean
of crabgrass; dandelions
extracted by their teeth,
and not a single pad of moss
along the sprayed drives
sealed like secrets.

But here rises one
neither sowed nor mowed
with grass you could part
with both hands,
a front lot filled
with rippling thistle
shepherd's purse, purple
vetch and quitch waving tall
around a pool turned olive
with twitching mosquitoes
as frogs speak late
into an evening
of abundant birds.

In a world of show gardens
staged showings
virtual tours

and handwriting
that says yes,
as it follows the line
to this end. A postscript:
We stayed home.
My mother survived;
this was freedom.

Allison A. deFreese
Portland, Oregon

White Screen

I can go three movies more a day from salty, tart
to saccharine, slacking till my head draws a blank.
Till jingles for children soothe into
a land of curves and curls, an instinct to start over
black & white. An artist's in a mother's life:
mask chemicals with onion soup.
She dims her kitchen back to a dark room.
Her son who suffered
an explosion takes shape in a pan.
A deserter saves a widow's daughter
on the other side with all he knows
of their anthem. His neighbor snipes his nape
in error. For rabbit stew, chef plays hunter
coaxing ferrets to the ground.
I want to agree with After on a yard
makeover, the clean slate a hedged verandah,
the fresh door bluebird-blue if refuge
is real. My halluces fit at the drought's most humid.
If I keep flipping, my signal should pick up snow—
not a bleached stage
for a bloodbath, no metaphor on a bleak future
but August 5th on Esquiline hill, mist me
a miracle mousse, cushion to break a fall,
an immaculate carpet made of flurries, for ash,
show me the slush that keeps slipping back
as flakes descending on a silent night,
score settled like a phantom
horseman with his head back on, enough
for the ill to stay in, disremember, to be beyond
again, my smallest, gills in a silver lake.

Kris Falcon
Metro Manila, Philippines

The Plains

Bouquet of seeds, from seeds.
Bouquet of frost, from buffalo.
Something that smells of sulfur, flares.
Wax, like hogs, dries on hooks.
Bouquet of June berries, from tablets.
Apples still grow on trees like sisters.
& sisters, like spiders, keep their trappings.
Bouquet of lung & root.
Kissed relics dropped in mailslots.
Bouquet of wheat-gold & thyme,
filtering conflicted virgins through tall grasses
to grains of shade, shades of love.
O great valve, O beloved meathook—
bring more bouquets to me:
of foxes, pheasants, & hunters
in equal measure. A wreath of nettles
for every door. Single stems
of tin, wren, & spade for every corner.
Smaller bouquets of cinnamon & stars.
Bouquets of heaven, lace, & bread.
A wrist-corsage of swing & arch
for me. A boutonniere for you—
all rope-knot & comet.

Micah Ruelle
Minneapolis, Minnesota

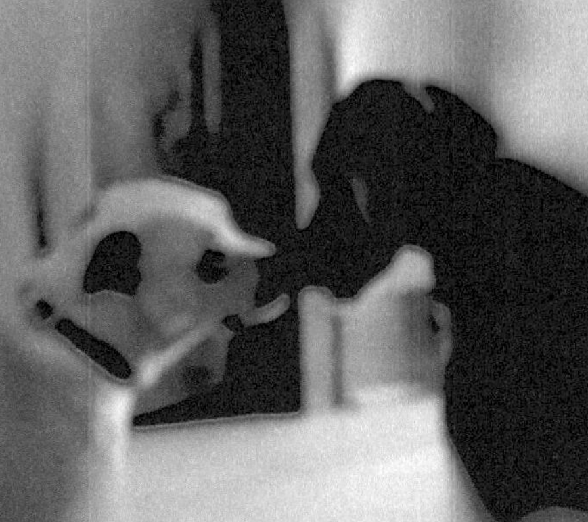

Trust your instincts.

Subscribe to *Plainsongs*.

Please visit our website at corpuscallosumpress.
com/plainsongs to subscribe via credit/debit
card, PayPal, or check.

Our 2022 rates:
- One-year e-subscription ($10)
- One-year print subscription ($25)
- Individual print issues available for $15

Questions? Contact the editor at
etucker@corpuscallosumpress.com or write to us:

Corpus Callosum Press
PO Box 1563
Hastings, NE 68902